THE ART OF
BILLY STRAYHORN

By David Pearl

Cover photo by William P. Gottlieb

Cherry Lane Music Company
Educational Director/Project Supervisor: Susan Poliniak
Director of Publications: Mark Phillips
Publications Coordinator: Rebecca Skidmore

ISBN 978-1-60378-034-6

Visit our website at www.cherrylaneprint.com

TABLE OF CONTENTS

INTRODUCTION

Billy Strayhorn's contributions as a composer, arranger, and pianist are as yet not fully appreciated by many in the world of jazz, fans and musicians included. His artistic profile has been obscured by his collaborative role with Duke Ellington and his willing (or reluctant) acceptance of a life lived behind the scenes. Most of the compositions he is known for became synonymous with the Ellington orchestra, the orchestra's musicians, and with Ellington himself. The door of opportunity opened, and Strayhorn became an architect of the Duke Ellington sound, a task he performed so transparently that even his independent achievements were inevitably associated with Ellington.

Strayhorn was born in 1915 in Dayton, Ohio and moved with his family to Pittsburgh in 1920, where he would live until moving to New York in 1939. His family was poor, but he took the initiative in studying the piano as a child. In his formative high school years, his teachers gave him lessons in piano and harmony, and the opportunity to perform and compose for the school's ensembles. After graduating, he enrolled at the Pittsburgh Musical Institute, but left the school when, during his second semester, his favorite teacher died. Strayhorn found gigs playing in local clubs while he worked at a drugstore until the chance came to meet and play for Ellington in late 1938. Clearly, he was a gifted and observant learner.

Strayhorn contributed compositions, arrangements, and lyrics, and covered the occasional piano part for the Duke Ellington Orchestra. He helped Ellington with his many writing projects, including the long-form suites and movies with which Ellington was credited. Though Strayhorn did venture out on his own on more than one occasion, he always returned to his collaborative relationship inside the Ellington organization.

A heavy smoker and drinker, Strayhorn developed cancer of the esophagus in 1964, and died in 1967, 51 years old and his body spent. The abundant praise from those who knew and worked with him is consistent in naming his personal dignity, brilliant musicianship, and the respect he engendered.

Billy Strayhorn developed his musical language at an early age, first adapting the extended chordal harmony of the French impressionist composers (Debussy, Ravel), and then, after discovering jazz, incorporating the sounds he heard from swing bands (Benny Goodman, Fletcher Henderson), the more sophisticated progressive sound of the Ellington Orchestra, and, the emerging, more pared-down style of bebop. His compositional approach was one of the most advanced in jazz, yet astonishingly it took shape while he was still in high school.

His role in the Duke Ellington Orchestra can be viewed as both a singular situation where he became a part of one of the most creative and successful organizations in jazz, and as the force that enabled Ellington's success at the expense of Strayhorn's own independence and individual development. He was unfairly denied credit for many of his compositions and arrangements, yet he was generously taken care of by the Ellington family. Strayhorn was offered food and clothes, a place to live, musical assignments that included access to the most sophisticated jazz ensemble of the day, and national and international recognition from his first day on the job and throughout most of his career. It was no doubt a bargain with consequences, but considering the time in which he lived, his limelight-averse personality, the social and racial barriers he had to face as a gay African-American, and the nature of the music business, perhaps it is difficult to look back and judge the overall fairness. The musical careers of both men were intertwined, their personalities complementary, linked by mutual need and defined by collaboration.

This book takes an in-depth look at Billy Strayhorn's art through five well-known and highly prized songs, and analyzes the form, melody, harmony, rhythm, and lyrics of each. Examples of interpretation by various performers—including Strayhorn, Ellington, and many other musicians—follow each analysis. An arrangement of each song is printed at the end of each chapter. Strayhorn's influences, techniques, and stylistic traits are identified and explained through musical examples so that those drawn to his music can gain a more complete and individual portrait of one of jazz's most important musicians.

ABOUT THE AUTHOR

David Pearl is the author of *The Art of Steely Dan* and *Color Your Chords for Keyboards*, a survey of the harmonic styles of 25 top jazz, blues, new age, and rock pianists. His many other books for Cherry Lane include jazz transcriptions of the artists Grover Washington, Jr., Dave Douglas, and McCoy Tyner, as well as arrangements of classical pieces and opera arias for piano. A freelance pianist, composer, and arranger, he lives in New York City with his wife and son, and performs and records regularly with singers and other instrumentalists. His recent projects include recording a CD of piano four-hands music with his wife, and developing and recording a series of piano lessons for the new online music education website WorkshopLive.

ACKNOWLEDGMENTS

Thanks to Susan Poliniak for guiding this project. Thanks also to Ray Hubley, editor of *Billy Strayhorn: Lush Life*, for sharing his insights and information. I highly recommend the film (listed below) to those interested in learning, seeing, and hearing more on Billy Strayhorn's life and music. I also recommend the following indispensable books, which pioneered the recent research into Strayhorn's life and music.

- *Billy Strayhorn: Lush Life*, a film shown as part of the PBS series *Independent Lens,* directed by Robert S. Levi, 2007

- *Lush Life: A Biography of Billy Strayhorn* by David Hajdu (Farrar Straus Giroux, 1996)

- *Something to Live For: The Music of Billy Strayhorn* by Walter van de Leur (Oxford University Press, 2002)

TAKE THE "A" TRAIN

Written in 1939, shortly after Billy Strayhorn met Duke Ellington, "'A' Train" became the theme song for the Duke Ellington Orchestra. It's one of the top standards in any jazz player's book.

FORM

The AABA form is probably the most common in American popular song. Each of the four sections is eight measures long, creating a 32-bar form, with the B section—the bridge—acting as a contrast to A.

All of the A sections are the same in "'A' Train" except for the last two measures, which have harmonic or melodic material leading to the next section: either the second A, on to the bridge, or back to the top for another chorus (meaning another time through the entire AABA form).

On the original Duke Ellington Orchestra recording from 1941, the entire chorus is repeated three times, forming a larger, three-part structure comprised of the melody, solos, and a return of the melody to the end.

- Chorus 1 (melody with backgrounds, AABA)
- Chorus 2 (trumpet solo, AABA)
- Chorus 3 (trumpet solo with backgrounds, AAB, and melody, A)

Including the introduction, transition, ending, and key changes, here is a detailed layout of the form.

> Key of C:
> Four-bar intro
> Chorus 1 (AABA)
>
> Key of C:
> Chorus 2—Muted trumpet solo (AABA)
>
> Four-bar transition to E♭
>
> Key of E♭:
> Chorus 3—Open (mute out) trumpet solo alternating with sax's chromatic riff (AA)
> Solo with trombone background (B) for six measures
> Two measures featuring an ensemble chord pyramid
> A—Played three times
> Ending

The very last A section, played softer with each repeat, acts as a coda, ending with the saxophone riff up the scale to the tonic.

The 32-bar AABA form has been a mainstay of jazz, and is usually placed in an overall structure of intro, melody ("head"), solos over AABA, melody ("head"), and ending.

RHYTHM

The all-important rhythmic underpinning of the song is in the steady, eight-to-the-bar beat of the swing eighth notes. In a medium-bright tempo, just right for big-band–style dancing, the rhythm evokes excitement, suspense, and . . . trains.

When we take a look at a boogie pattern, there are three elements that apply to "Take the 'A' Train": constant eighth note motion, alternating up-down-up intervals, and chromatic passing tones.

These elements mimic the momentum and motion of a train. Now look at the song's melodic "signature," starting in measure 6 of the A section.

The same three elements are at work, pushing the momentum of the song forward.

This boogie-style momentum is achieved in the rhythmic motion of the melody, which rides on the underlying swing rhythm. The melodic rhythm of the A section builds as it develops over the eight measures. Measures 1–5 set up these boogie eighths in measures 6 and 7 by building up the energy through the long-held, chromatically ascending notes.

The syncopated rhythm in bar 2 is used as an organizing principle for the entire piece. Approached by either an upward leap or a downward drop, the dotted quarter note that comes off the downbeat is a feature throughout the song, notably in the intro; bars 2, 3, and 7 of the A sections; bars 1–3 and 5–7 of the bridge; and the ending riff. Combined with the steady eighth note pulse, these syncopations create a vibrant rhythmic texture.

We can find more of these syncopations in the backgrounds that fill in spaces behind the melody. They also use the same rhythmic punches.

The four-bar transition to E♭ features a four-against-three rhythm (a hemiola-like pattern of four dotted half notes over three four-beat measures) breaking up the steady four-beat pattern before re-establishing the beat for the third chorus.

MELODY

The melody is also characterized by upward leaps and downward drops. These all grow out of the jump of a major 6th in the second measure. Following the melody on through the A section, we find three other jumps of either major or minor 6ths. This is then "expanded" in the bridge, with intervallic jumps of major and minor 7ths. Clearly, these large intervals are a key melodic device throughout. Yet it is the chromatic motion of the melody that shows Billy Strayhorn's greatest gifts as a composer. A detailed look shows that every note in the melody has a function, pushing forward to a note of resolution.

From the first note, we can see that the lower line of the melody creeps chromatically upward to the leading tone, B, before plunging downward—again, chromatically—from G to E. Looking at the upper notes, the high E holds out until, moving in tandem with the lower notes, there's a downward dive to the tonic. Put together, these lines move in on the tonic from both sides, a squeeze effect that makes the melody so satisfying.

Now, let's look for similar lines in the bridge.

The starting note, A, functions as the "median," while above and below the chromatic lines close in, all forcing the resolution down to A♭ and then to G, the starting note for the A section.

The melody notes of the bridge outline a major 7th chord (Fmaj7) for the first four bars, and then a D9 (minus the root) for the next four bars. The melodic use of the 7th interval is a feature in many of Strayhorn's other pieces such as "Chelsea Bridge," "Isfahan," and "Johnny Come Lately."

The chromatic encircling of a note points to one of the important melodic influences on Billy Strayhorn: bebop. Circling in on a chord note from its chromatic neighbors—a very common gesture in the playing of bebop pioneers such as Charlie Parker and Dizzy Gillespie—looks something like this.

Strayhorn seems to construct the melody to "Take the 'A' Train" with notes that similarly circle in as they resolve.

Aiming to create his first big-band arrangement for Ellington's orchestra, Strayhorn was, naturally, influenced by arrangers he had listened to as a student. You can hear this in the original "'A' Train" arrangement. The sax section plays the opening melody in unison, with the brass section filling in with rhythmic chordal punches. This is a similar treatment given to Benny Goodman's 1935 hit "Don't Be That Way," arranged by Edgar Sampson.

And could it be that Strayhorn's whole tone melody in the piano intro was influenced by Claude Debussy?

The melodic riff that ends the song reverses the chromatic motion ending the A section, leading back up to the 5th, then up to the root.

For a great example of economy, Strayhorn uses these same upward-leading notes in the four-bar transition to E♭, this time starting on G (the 5th of the key of C) moving up to B♭ (the 5th of the new key, E♭) with the rhythm elongated into the four-against-three hemiola.

HARMONY

The harmonic progression in "Take the 'A' Train" is, in contrast with most other Strayhorn compositions, a fairly conventional sequence of chords that stays very close to the home key.

The A-section progression is a bedrock progression of the swing era, starting and ending on the I chord, with a jog to the II7 (or V7 of V) and a common ii–V–I to bring us home.

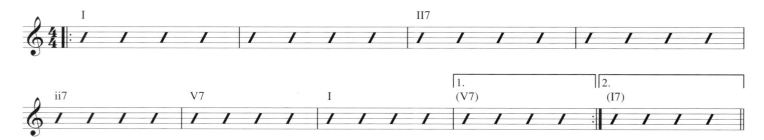

This type of progression can be found in songs such as Ellington's "Solitude" (1933) and "Mood Indigo" (1930), where the progression is contracted to four measures. The unusual element in "'A' Train" is found in the third measure, when the melody drops down from the 9th of the II chord to the ♯11th. This trait of tracing the melody along the upper extensions of the harmony is true to Strayhorn's style, and one that we will see in all his other compositions.

The B section begins, by way of the I7 in the measure before, with the IV chord, a temporary modulation. Here, the melody again stresses an upper extension—this time, the major 7th of the IV chord, then the 9th of the II7 chord, and finally the ♭9th of the V7 chord.

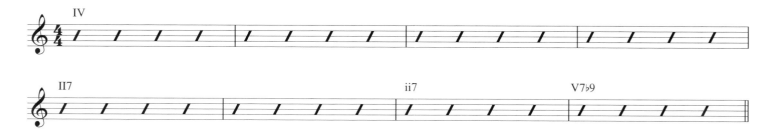

We should note the connection between the II7♯11 in measures 3 and 4 of the A section and the same chord used in the introduction. Its rich, biting sound is derived from the whole tone scale, which is frequently used in backgrounds, fills, and solos over this chord.

When voiced across the brass section, answering the single-note melody of the saxes, the harmony makes a nice allusion to the sound of a train whistle. There is a similar example of this in Ellington's 1933 "Daybreak Express," with its portrayal of a train whistle in a sequence of chromatically descending 13th and ♯11 chords, a device which became emblematic of the Ellington sound.

LYRICS

Strayhorn's lyrics to the song are of a certain place and time—that of the Harlem Renaissance of the 1920s and 1930s. With many of the top jazz artists and jazz clubs in the area, Harlem was the focal point of jazz in 1939.

After Billy Strayhorn first met Duke in 1938, Ellington gave Strayhorn directions to visit him in New York City. To get to Ellington's apartment, Strayhorn was told to take the "A" train, the subway line that runs express through Manhattan and stops at 145th and 155th streets, the southern and northern borders of the Sugar Hill neighborhood where Duke Ellington lived. While the B and C lines make local stops along the way and the D train veers east from 145th, the A train is the "quickest." The song lyrics offer a simple retelling of these directions, with the bridge adding in the element of excitement.

With the syllables matching the eighth note motion of the rhythm, the lyrics help convey the motion of the train, with the band adding the whistle hoots as background.

"Hurry—get on now." These lyrics open the bridge with such freshness and excitement that the function of the section—to provide contrast—is immediately felt.

"Listen to those rails a-thrumming." Here is an excellent example of unusual wordplay to make a clever and musical rhyme, with the added feature of the onomatopoeic "thrumming."

"All 'board" mimics the conductor's cry as a train leaves the station.

INTERPRETATION

"Take the 'A' Train" has been performed and recorded so many times that discussions of the various interpretations could take up an entire book. Let's look at a few of the more common interpretive additions.

Many singers and instrumentalists do not articulate the ♭9th of the melody at the end of measure 6, which resolves to the root in measure 7 of all A sections, and instead sing or play the ♮9th.

The saxophone riff with a chromatic run that alternates with Ray Nance's trumpet solo on the original 1941 recording is often played on the last of a series of solo choruses.

Nance's trumpet solo on the original recording was so widely admired that it became a standard "alternate" melody to play over the chord progression. Here is how Billy Strayhorn's group did the first 16 measures for their recording.

During the bridge, rhythm sections use these parallel chromatic passing chords in the fourth measure, from the IV chord down to the II7.

Singers—and anyone else wanting some tips on improvising—might learn from one of Ella Fitzgerald's turns on the melody. It's a marvel of variation and invention. This is from her last chorus on one of her recordings of the tune.

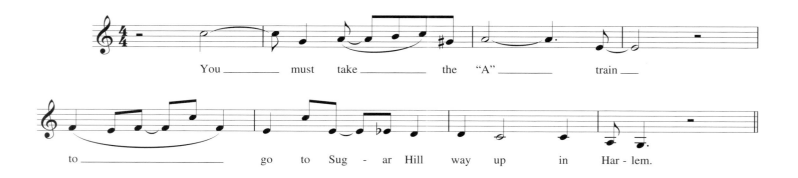

TAKE THE "A" TRAIN

Words and Music by
Billy Strayhorn

CHELSEA BRIDGE

One of Strayhorn's most hauntingly beautiful ballads, "Chelsea Bridge" (1941), is unique in its lyricism.

FORM

In its overall design, the song has several features in common with Duke Ellington's "In a Sentimental Mood"(1935), a 4/4 ballad that also has a 32-measure AABA form. The songs share a three-beat ascending eighth note pickup to a whole note in a minor key, and use melody notes that land and are held on upper chord extensions. With a winding melody among minor-chord harmonies in the opening four measures, the A sections both cadence simply on the tonic of relative major. Both songs also explore a remote major key in the bridge, with flowing melodic movement and brighter harmonies.

Key Relationships

"In a Sentimental Mood"

- A section: Starting in D minor, ending in F (relative major)
- B section: Modulation to D♭ major (major 3rd below tonic F), leading into the V7 of F for the last A.

"Chelsea Bridge"

- A section: Starting in B♭ minor, ending in D♭ (relative major)
- B section: Modulation to E major (minor 3rd above tonic D♭), then to A major (major 3rd below tonic D♭), then briefly G major to G minor, leading to C7 (V7 of F), which points back to B♭ minor for the last A.

At the end of the bridge of each song, the melody, harmony, and rhythm break on the first beat of the eighth measure, for the pickup to the last A. Both songs also make use of the minor-major 7th chord—a rarity for the time.

The introduction and ending are not significant formal features, since "Chelsea Bridge" is so dense. It is a challenge to set up the initial pickup, since the harmonic framework must be set before the ascending scale. Among the various options that have been used, Duke Ellington set up the original arrangement with a quick three-measure piano solo in B♭ minor, ending with a Cm7♭5 (ii7 of the opening key). Billy Strayhorn often set up the song with an extended, rhythmically free riff on the relative major, D♭.

Endings are typically very brief. The ending used in the arrangement at the end of this chapter uses a Strayhornesque parallel progression a half step above the tonic, resolving back to the tonic for the final measure. This has the advantage of simplicity and of summarizing the many half step motifs heard in the melody.

MELODY

The A-section melody opens with a rising line up the natural minor scale, pushing finally up a half step to a non-chord note, the major 7th of the B♭m chord. This is the first of many important melody notes that highlight an upper extension chord note. In the A section alone, the melody emphasizes the major 7th, 9th, and 11th of the various harmonies. As if soothing the chromaticism of the opening few measures, the last four bars simplify and solidify the switch from minor to relative major, using the notes of the home-key D♭ triad.

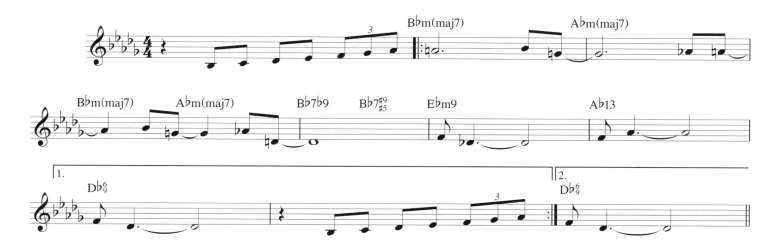

Continuing into the bridge, the melody moves from the tonic up to the 5th of the key, Ab, becoming G♯, the common note between the key of Db and the new key, E major. The melody here in the bridge also emphasizes the upper chord-note extensions, particularly the 11th, b9th, ♯11th, and ♯13th.

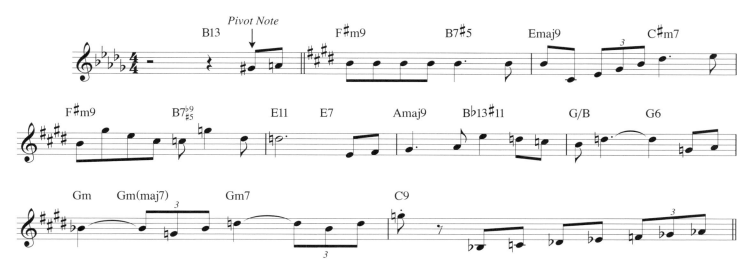

The abundant chromaticism—apparent in nearly every measure here—is a feature of Billy Strayhorn's melodic writing. Melodic cells or motifs are expanded and developed, stretching into intervals that carry the sound of jazz, colorful alterations of complex harmonies.

The A-section melody develops a motif using the intervals of a rising half step and a falling minor 3rd.

Follow the development through the section as the intervals replicate and expand into a tritone (two minor 3rds down) and then a resolution on a descending major 3rd. At the same time, the lower note of the tritone, D♮, is resolved a half step down to the tonic, Db. So within these eight measures, the motif is introduced, developed, and resolved.

This illustrates Strayhorn's economy of means—the way he sticks to a two-note motif throughout the entire A section, yet builds drama into the structure by developing the motif all the way through the eight-measure section. A contrast is apparent, then, with Ellington's "In a Sentimental Mood," which has longer melodic lines that flow in a soothing manner, more uniform in character and without the dramatic dimension. In "Chelsea Bridge," the very reticence of the melody gives it intensity along with an introspective, haunting mystery.

The bridge provides a release from the minimalist constraints of the A section, with a much higher range, modulations with fresh harmonic changes, and a melody more improvisational and instrumental in nature. As in a sax riff, the melody traces the chord changes, hitting upon the upper extensions especially. As in "'A' Train," Strayhorn's melody circles the key notes that signal a harmonic change, approaching from both below and above, marking the new harmonic territory using nearly all of the notes in the chromatic scale.

Even though the bridge contrasts the A section in many respects, it is unified by the same compositional means. Melodically, it also emphasizes half steps and minor 3rds, as in the opening motif.

HARMONY

In addition to the similarities in overall design, the A-section chord progression of "Chelsea Bridge" bears some similarity to that of "In a Sentimental Mood." Both use the change from the i minor to I7 as a way to pivot to the relative major, with the I7 becoming the VI7 of the relative major, continuing on into a ii7–V7–I cadence.

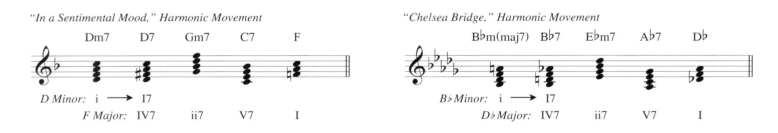

Beyond these similarities, the exploitation of the ripest harmonies is more characteristic of Strayhorn's compositions than of Ellington's. In fact, the parallel minor-major 7th chords in the first three measures are quite unique to jazz tunes of the time, and have more in common with the harmonic progressions of Ravel and Debussy.

Maurice Ravel, Valses nobles et sentimentales, *Number 2, Measures 17–20*

Parallel chords are used in "Lush Life" and "Passion Flower," too; the opening progression in "Chelsea Bridge" may be viewed as a minor-key variation of the D♭–C♭ back-and-forth progression opening of "Lush Life." The harmony here is more ambiguous and reluctant to commit to a tonal direction until measure 4.

Strayhorn created complex, five- and six-note chords that give deep, mysterious colors to the backgrounds.

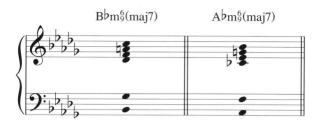

These chords are rich with interval combinations, the stacked 3rds creating polychords that, in parallel motion, are imbued with an ambiguous, tidal feeling.

It's worth noting the key relationships at work throughout the song, and how they're tied to the melodic motifs. In particular, the use of the minor 3rd in the melodic motif is echoed in the relationship between the relative minor and relative major (B♭ minor to D♭ major) and the tonic to the modulation at the bridge (D♭ major to E major).

The pattern of descending whole step modulations that fills the remaining measures of the bridge (A to G, heading to F) echoes the opening parallel progression down a whole step.

This "heading to F" makes sense as bringing the harmony back to B♭ minor, with F7 as pivot (V of B♭m). C7 is the V of F, with C♭7 as the tritone substitute for F7, leading chromatically down to B♭m as the melody ascends.

RHYTHM

Because it is an atmospheric, gentle ballad, the rhythmic interest of "Chelsea Bridge" is away from the smooth, slow, background of the bass and drums. Rather, the focus is on the melodic rhythm, with the theme leading the way. The ascending pickup, a combination of eighth notes and a triplet at the end, emerges into a defining pattern: a long-held note followed by a single short note, quickly changing into another long note in a new mode. The simplicity of the rhythmic pattern is the defining aspect of the theme.

After this rhythm is introduced and repeated in the opening measures, the same rhythmic unit is displaced, with the emphasis moved from the syncopation before the downbeat to the downbeat itself.

This now moves the focus onto the shorter note and away from the longer note, and creates a more settled pattern to go with the gently consonant melodic line, gliding to a resolution in measure 7. This rhythmic design is the opposite of that in "'A' Train," where the rhythmic momentum slowly builds throughout the A section, releasing the tension in the active sixth measure.

To contrast the quiet, schematic rhythms of the A section, the rhythmic motion of the bridge flows freely in the melody, as the development of eighth notes and triplets unfolds improvisationally. There is really no rhythmic repetition in the bridge, save for the seventh measure, which sets up the pickup returning to the A section.

The rhythmic break in measure 8, leaving the melody spotlighted with no rhythmic or harmonic accompaniment, is very important in returning to the more austere feeling of the closing A section.

LYRICS

Inspired by an impressionist-style painting by English artist James McNeill Whistler that portrays the bridge at dusk with London's Thames River flowing underneath, "Chelsea Bridge" is a mood piece perfectly suited for an instrumental interpretation. Yet the haunting and lyrical melody has inspired the wordless vocalise of Sarah Vaughn, Ella Fitzgerald, Dianne Reeves, and Cassandra Wilson.

Lena Horne, one of Billy Strayhorn's closest friends, sang the following lyric in her recording:

> Once again I go to Chelsea Bridge,
> A place that calls to me.
> Where I found my lover
> In the solitude of misty nights,
> Where fog deserts the sea.
> Looking for my lover
> In the early days of spring when love was young,
> We were children dancing through the clouds up on high.
> But the light of spring turned to winter,
> Love grew old, and again it's last goodbye.
> In my loneliness, I wait and pray
> My love will come to me,
> Back to Chelsea Bridge.

On this version, which features the beautiful accompaniment of Herbie Hancock on piano, the bridge is transposed down a 5th from its written relationship to the A sections. This makes the range of the melody much more manageable for a singer.

INTERPRETATION

As with so many Strayhorn tunes, variations abound in different recordings and performances. With the character of the melody on the bridge already improvisational, most of the melodic variation occurs here. But some variations of the A section melody are also common.

On the Duke Ellington Orchestra recordings, and others, the ending cadence was often played in the following two ways.

Ben Webster's seminal performances often included this catchy melodic variation in measures 3 and 4.

Harmonic variations—on the A-section, turnaround, and B-section chords—are also common. The first two chords are often altered by keeping the upper chord structure and adding a new bass note, creating a progression from E♭9♯11 to D♭9, as can be heard in some Ben Webster recordings.

There are several possibilities for harmonizing the ascending melodic pickup. Here are two common progressions, both of which lead to the relative minor.

In the bridge, measures 5–8 are played with various chord changes. There is an additional melodic variation leading chromatically into the G minor chord in this section.

Although this is mostly performed as a slow ballad, there are many versions that have a medium-swing or Latin rhythm feel. The Duke Ellington Orchestra recording of 1941 features a moderate, "dance band," swing tempo, not nearly as slow as most later versions of the song. Ella Fitzgerald, singing with the orchestra, inserted a Latin-flavored beat with tom-toms under the first four measures. This rhythm was used in many other recordings as well.

CHELSEA BRIDGE

By Billy Strayhorn

PASSION FLOWER

"Passion Flower" (1940) is a perfect example of how a unified composition is created from a single motif. All of the melodic and harmonic material is built from the opening three notes. This compositional unity and economy of means is achieved by the organic development of a motif throughout the melody, bass line, and inner voice-leading of the harmony.

FORM

"Passion Flower," like "Chelsea Bridge," is cast in a traditional AABA form, and in every respect the formal concept is paramount. Using a three-note motif similar to "Chelsea Bridge," Strayhorn created an even tighter composition in which every aspect grows out of this motif. Most importantly, he skillfully introduces and guides tension by developing organically from the opening motif and keeping tight control over it throughout the form. Each section has its own level of tension and release, with the climax reaching full power at the peak of the bridge.

Both the A and B sections are created with the simplest of means, showing an economy worthy of Beethoven. Scrutinize the relationship of intervals in the opening three-note melodic motif and you'll find all of the elements used throughout the entire composition.

Let's start by analyzing the introduction, which uses material from the last measure of the A sections. Even though it's just a brief two measures, it shouldn't be overlooked: It creates a setting for the tonal center and establishes the voicing for the melody, bass, and inner voices. This is crucial because the A section starts on a tonally ambiguous point.

In the full piano/vocal arrangement that follows this discussion, the two-measure intro also serves the composition by introducing the chromatic nature of the song.

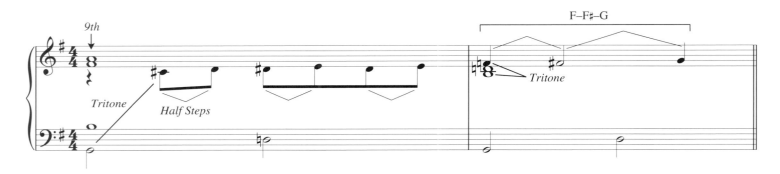

The opening chord, on beat 1, establishes the key of G major, with the 9th in the top voice establishing the melodic focus, and capturing the jazzy Strayhorn sound. This is important, as it is also the note of resolution in the melody. The tritone, from G to C♯, is heard as the first note of the ascending chromatic line, entering on beat 2. Tritone relationships play a crucial role, binding the melody and harmony throughout.

The chromatic line then establishes a pattern of two-note half step rises, which leads to the surprising F♮ on the downbeat of the second measure. This is important for four reasons: it brings the non-diatonic note of F into play, melodically, preparing for its appearance in the bridge; it brings another tritone relationship into play, with the 3rd of the G chord (B) a tritone below; it establishes an important pattern of relative consonance, where the three-note F–F♯–G figure places the emphasis on beats 1 and 2, and displaces what would ordinarily be the note of resolution, the tonic G, to the weakest beat; and then these three chromatic notes are then taken up in retrograde in the bass line, starting with the G in the introduction and continuing with F♯ to F♮ as the first two chordal roots. This chromatically descending bass line sets the character for the bass throughout the composition.

MELODY

In the A section, the melodic outline shows the overall movement three notes down, from C to B to A, (in the key of G major, the 4th to the 3rd to the 2nd), and three notes up (an exact inversion) in the B section, from F to G♭ to A♭ (in the key of D♭ major, the 3rd to the 4th to the 5th).

A-Section Outline

B-Section Outline

Within this three-note outline are three-note motifs: the first, up a major 2nd, down a minor 3rd, with the general focus on the outline of a minor 2nd down, C to B. This minor 2nd down, in measures 1 and 2, is paralleled in the bass line at the interval of a tritone. The tritone in the bass maintains the tension, pulling away from the natural tendency for the C-to-B to sound like a resolution.

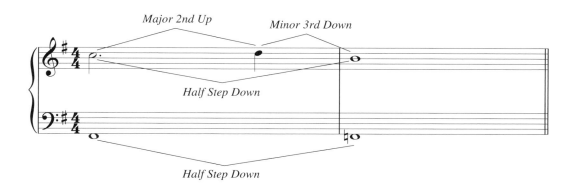

With a bit of rhythmic variation, this is repeated in measures 3 and 4, and then the motif is expanded while the bass line climbs lower by half steps. The rise of a major 2nd in the first two notes of the melodic cell is expanded to a minor 3rd, from there expanding the interval down to the B, a major 3rd. The entire motif is then extended in a similar pattern, with the final downward drop finally a 4th down to the A—overall, an incremental expansion of intervals. Yet, in addition to the opening three notes, only two more notes are added to the entire A section, with an overall feeling of tension easing slightly to resolution.

The three-note pickup to the bridge reverses the pattern of falling intervals and ascends the G major triad, for the first time—and only briefly—outlining the home key. Up to this point, Strayhorn established the 9th of the chord, A, as the note of resolution for the A section. In traditional harmony, this A is unresolved until it falls to the root, G. Yet the first instance of a chordal root in the melody is here, at the pickup to the bridge! Just as soon, however, the melody jumps up the G major triad, and from the 5th, D, another minor 3rd to F♮. In addition to outlining a G7 chord, this bold new note arrives with a bolder harmonic choice: a direct modulation to the key of D♭. But both the melody note and the chord have been prepared organically from within the composition: The F♮ from the intro and first ending line, and the D♭ because of the omnipresent tritone relationship, now revealed as part of the structural design between the A and B sections.

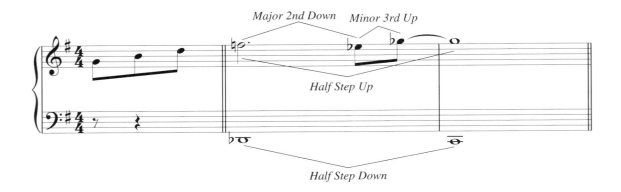

From the start of the bridge, the A section motif is inverted: from the F, a major 2nd down, followed by a minor 3rd up. The melodic rhythm is similar to that of the A section, outlining in essence the movement up a half step from F to G♭. Following the development of the melody here, we can see the melodic outline of the B section as three notes mirroring that of the A section, building the tension, and reaching a climax on the highest note. Again, it's worth noting that this is achieved with so few notes and such minimal variation.

The melodic movement of the bass line, as in the A section, is downward in half steps, from the D♭ down to the dominant, A♭, resolving back to the tonic D♭. In a one-beat summation, the chromatically descending chords in measure 8 of the bridge echo the movement of the bass line, though down one step, setting up the return to the A section.

The melody then takes up the chromatic motif of the bass line, starting from the E on the final beat of the bridge down to the C at the start of the last A section. The interesting thing about this E is that it is the median between the final, climactic note of the bridge (high A♭) and the C that begins the A section—in other words, chromatically down four notes from the A♭. This all points to the fact that in a fully integrated compositional style, the melodic and harmonic material can't be completely separated.

HARMONY

In the 1930s there were other examples of songs that pushed the envelope, chromatically speaking. Ellington's "Sophisticated Lady" and the melody to Peter De Rose's "Deep Purple" come to mind. Strayhorn seems to have taken his cue from these songs to explore further. For example, there is a notable connection to the chromatically descending chord progression of "Sophisticated Lady." Compare the similarities in the A section harmonies of "Sophisticated Lady" (measures 1–3, transposed to G) and "Passion Flower" (measures 3–7).

Yet "Passion Flower" breaks new ground for the chromatic nature of the melodic movement and harmonic and melodic content. The melodic movement is chromatic, the harmonic structures feature the tritone. Within the spectrum of relative consonance and dissonance, the interval of a tritone is generally most dissonant, and is resolved with one or both of the notes moving chromatically to a more consonant, stable interval. Yet it is heard throughout the harmony of "Passion Flower," and without the usual harmonic resolution. Here we can examine in more detail the tritone relationships: within chord structure (root to ♭5th, 3rd to 7th), bass line to melody, tonal centers between sections, and in the melodic nature of the bass line and inner voices. So Strayhorn is achieving a rather unique feat with this progression. He is carefully calibrating the resolution to the tonic through a series of complex and subtle harmonic and melodic relationships.

As noted earlier, the bass line has its own melody. It starts with G in the intro, and descends chromatically down to the V chord. This same line, transposed to D♭, can be found in the bridge, where it begins on I (D♭maj7) and continues down to the V7 of the key (A♭7). The chromatic fill on the last beat of the bridge not only extends the downward line—it also ends on G, anticipating the start of the last A section as the intro did for the first A. When the bass line is isolated, the melodic nature of the writing and its connection to the melody itself become clear.

With the downward movement of the bass line established, we can then follow the inner voices that fill in the harmony. With some interesting exceptions in the position of the 9th of the chord, the voicings move parallel to the bass line, all the way into the resolution of the Gmaj9. In bars 4 and 5, the top line moves independently, creating a more contrapuntal texture. This independent movement of the top harmonic voice adds an extra richness, a dimension gained because the progression isn't entirely in parallel motion.

The featured chord, a 7th with a ♭5th and added 9th, has two tritones built into its makeup: from the root to the ♭5th, and from the 3rd to the 7th. The chord can be derived from the whole-tone scale, which has three pairs of tritone-related notes.

The A9♯5 in the bridge is also based on the whole-tone scale.

The other altered 9ths—the B♭7$^{♭9}_{♯5}$ in the bridge and the D7$^{♯9}_{♯5}$ at the coda—get their dissonant bite from the minor 9th and major 7th intervals in addition to the tritones.

And the sequence of descending ♭5 chords at the end of the bridge is also made out of a pair of tritones.

RHYTHM

Long note vs. short, syncopated vs. unsyncopated—the rhythmic features of the song also follow simple characteristics. There are rhythmic features similar to "Chelsea Bridge." The use of quarter note triplets provides tension in its three-against-four pull. The mix of rhythms in the melody is offset by the smooth blanket of half and whole notes in the harmony. Contrast to the overall smoothness is provided by fast-moving harmony in eighth and 16th notes at the end of the bridge.

As regards an overall description: smooth and placid, with just enough syncopation and cross rhythm to keep tension palpable just below the surface. The tensions are usually sudden and brief, returning quickly to a smooth rhythmic background. The pattern established by the melodic rhythm is characterized by long notes under which the rhythm stays smooth, abruptly broken by brief wrinkles in the rhythmic pattern, and followed by a return to the longer, smoother tones.

At the same time, the rhythm of the harmonic movement stays subtly even and smooth: the momentum toward the resolution in measure 7 is given a slight push by the half note movement of the upper voice of the harmony. And in the bridge, the rhythmic motion of the chords underneath the melody in measures 7 and 8 works quickly to deflate the huge climax of the melody.

LYRICS

"Passion Flower," "A Flower Is a Lovesome Thing," "Ballad for Very Tired and Sad Lotus Eaters," "Blossom," "Blue Orchid," "Jasmine," "Lament for an Orchid," "Lotus Blossom," "Pussy Willow," "Rose Bud"—flowers fill the compositions of Billy Strayhorn. In the time he spent with his grandmother learning about flowers at her North Carolina home, and in his relationships with his mother Lillian Young and his partner Aaron Bridgers, flowers played an important role in his life.

The lyrics for this song were written by Milton Raskin, also a pianist and composer, who penned lyrics for another Strayhorn classic, "Day Dream." In making the flower-as-lover metaphor explicit, the lyric succeeds in matching the intimate, sensual atmosphere of the music.

INTERPRETATION

In the recordings Billy Strayhorn made of "Passion Flower," an important element is the considerable amount of lively filling, which counters the slow, silky smoothness of the melody and harmonic background. The slow, rich harmonies and languorous melody are counterbalanced by light grace note piano fills throughout and offbeat chordal pushes at the ends of choruses.

One of Strayhorn's small-group arrangements segues from a slow, ruminative feel into an up-tempo, bop-influenced feel with assertive chordal jabs. Strayhorn sets the new tempo with the piano playing double-time swing.

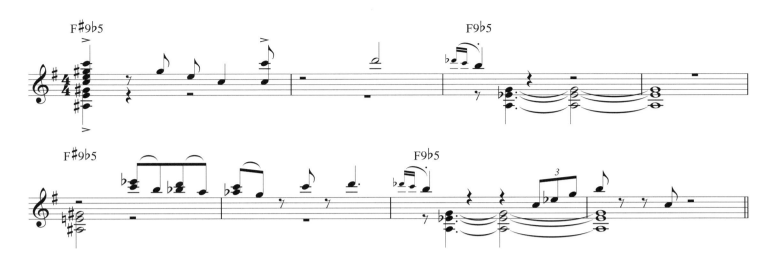

Showing effortless application of whole tone scales over the chords, Grover Washington starts his soprano sax solo with these riffs on his recording.

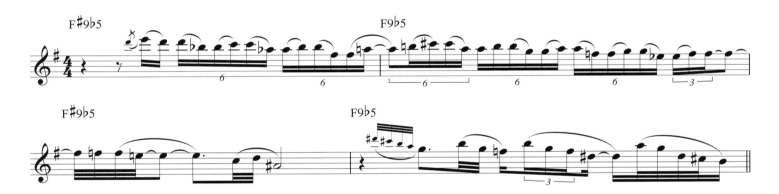

In another notable interpretation, Fred Hersch sets the tune as a jazz waltz on his recording, with every measure of the original divided into two measures of 3/4 time.

PASSION FLOWER

Words by Milton Raskin

Music by Billy Strayhorn

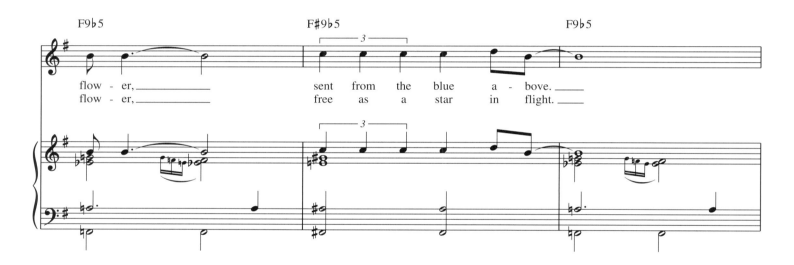

A FLOWER IS A LOVESOME THING

The organizing principle of this gorgeous 1939 ballad is as concise as it is simple: a half step. This concept is manifest in the opening melodic motif, the closing melodic motif, the bridge theme, and in the key relationships within the bridge and between the A and B sections.

FORM

The form is AABA, 32 measures, with an intro and coda. The A and B sections share an inner structure—both utilize a two-measure opening motif, repeated in measures 3 and 4, and a development of the motif in measures 5 through 8. In a sense, they are parallel rather than contrasting sections, although the B section is differentiated as the melody ascends and grows, brightening the darker feel of the A section. Similar in organic design to "Passion Flower," the B section emerges from the A section material, inverting the downward direction into an uplifting, ascending climax.

The half step relationship is also exploited in the harmony throughout, most obviously in the cadence of the resolution, where the chromatic progression II7–♭II–I, with the tonic in the melody, gives the song its characteristic beauty.

Using a standard and conventional form, Strayhorn makes his unique compositional statement with the creative development of small, tightly defined motifs that infuse the form through and through. The structure is held together through the emphasis of the half step interval.

The piano arrangement at the end of the chapter uses a four-measure intro from measures 5–8 of the A section. For the coda, the final two-measure theme is repeated, slowing to the final tonic resolution.

MELODY

A three-note grouping, based on the interval of a half step, is used throughout the song. First, in the A section, in measures 1 and 7.

And in the bridge, the same three-note group, in three places, emphasizing the half step in each group.

The opening motif, with the three-note grouping tucked inside, then becomes the theme of the A section. The melody is made of scale notes from the tonic, D♭, set to non-diatonic harmony, which puts the melody notes on upper chord extensions.

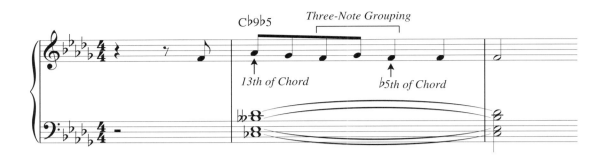

Working with this motif, Strayhorn builds a miniature three-part structure: the motif is introduced and repeated, the motif is developed and repeated in a parallel harmony, and a resolution—a "bookend" to the initial motif—leads to the tonic. Through this structure, with the half step interval as the building block, Strayhorn has worked chromatically downward to the root, D♭.

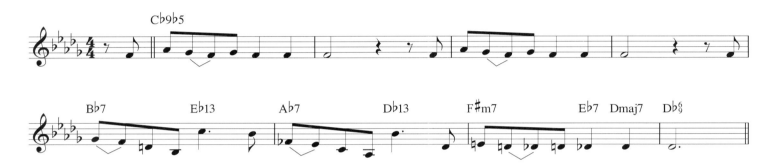

The B section begins with the half step motif now inching up from the 5th of the key, giving a "harmonic minor scale" impression. This motif emphasizes the jump up from A to C, a minor 3rd, which is an inversion of the minor 3rd outline of the A-section motif. This new motif, derived from the previous section, is then transposed up a half step for measures 3 and 4.

Then it is developed further, and the B motif is heard in its highest placement, with the minor 3rd now replaced by a more lyrical major 2nd up to the peak, E, and then down the D major triad, with the three-note motif leading back up to B♭. The B-section melodic structure is built with five variations on the half step interval.

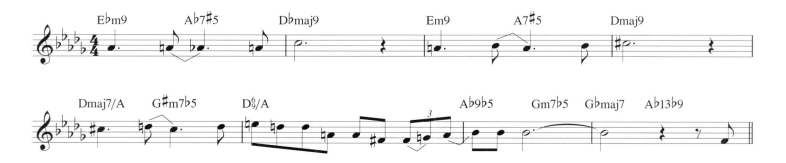

HARMONY

The focus of the harmonic design is on the relationship of the bass note to the melody. The A-section melodic motif rests on F, with the bass note, C♭, a tritone away, creating the unsettled, tonally ambiguous feeling, with the overall harmonic effect hinting at polytonality—a D♭ triad over C♭7.

The bass note and chord remain in this harmonic limbo for four full measures, when finally the bass note drops down—a half step! Continuing on in the progression, the melody lands on an extension when the chord and bass note change, creating a constant pull for the melody to evolve and move forward. The progression is a sequence, with the chord root moving in descending 5ths under a pattern of alternating 7th chords (briefly augmented by the melody) and 13th chords.

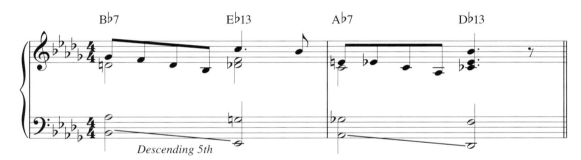

As in many of his other compositions, a resolution comes only at the end of the section. The resolution features chords in descending chromatic motion, echoing the descending half step motif in the melody.

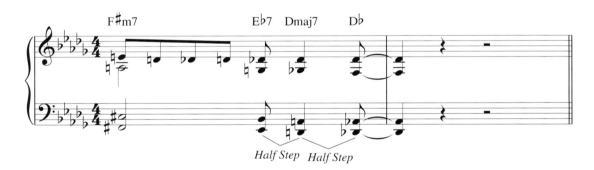

The harmony in the bridge plays with the half step relationship throughout. There is a straightforward ii–V–I in the first two measures, and then a modulation up a half step—the same progression and same melody transposed up to D. The inner voice adds another chromatic element, in contrary motion to the melody, from the 9th of ii to the ♯5th of V to the 9th of I.

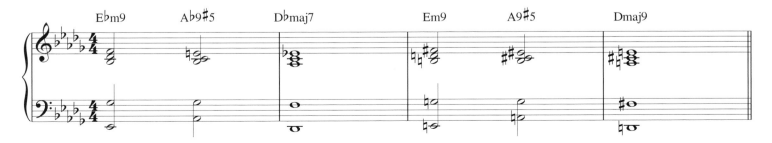

Then, something more unusual can be noticed: staying in the key of D, with the 5th degree, A, in the bass, like a pedal point, moving down a half step and then back up. This emphasizes the dominant (V7) of both keys as well as mirroring the half step melodic motif in the bass.

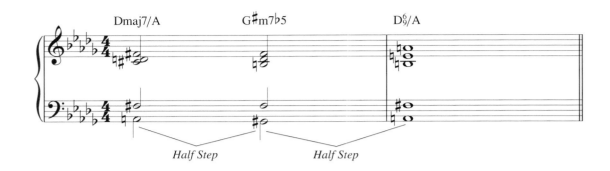

The transition chords continue the chromatic motion in measures 7 and 8. The Ab9b5—the tritone dominant chord of the key of D—sounds at first distant and unresolved, but after the key orientation of Db major has been prepared, this chord returns on the last two beats as the dominant for the return to the A section. Again, the harmonies create smooth, chromatic voice leading.

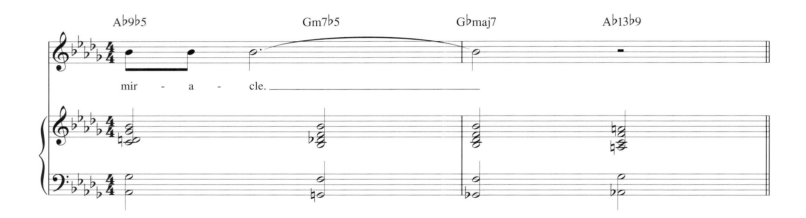

Notice how this Ab9b5 chord, ethereal in the context of D major, paints the word "miracle" in the lyrics, with the melody on the 9th of the chord. It lingers, otherworldly, until the harmony moves down and back again to re-establish the key of Db.

RHYTHM

The quiet stillness of the song means a more muted rhythmic setting, and a slow moving tempo. This allows the melody and harmony to inhabit the form without any sense of rushing. A floating, "out of time" feeling helps the mood in measures 1-4, and a stronger sense of time is established for measures 5–8, with the syncopations accenting the resolution into the final measure.

The melody demands a more colorful approach to rhythm during the bridge. As the melody climbs to a climax, it is not a loud one—rather, it is soft and understated. In his solo interpretation, Billy Strayhorn stops time, quietly, in measure 6, and picks it back up in measure 7.

There is an opportunity to take a more active approach to rhythm at times. A hint of bluesy swing can be given to the song, with the melody loosely phrased and allowing for variation in the repeated motifs. The eighth notes are usually phrased evenly during the first four measures, then more bluesy and with a swing in measures 5 to 8 of the A section.

LYRICS

Less likely than "Passion Flower" to be interpreted metaphorically, the lyric, with its devotion to the beauty of nature and the intoxicating allure of flowers, is an invitation to give oneself fully to the senses.

A flower is a lovesome thing
A luscious, living, lovesome thing
A daffodil, a rose
No matter where it grows
Is such a lovely, lovesome thing

A flower is the heart of spring
That makes the rolling hillside sing
The gentle winds that blow
Blow gently, for they know
A flower is a lovesome thing

Playing in the breeze
Swaying with the trees
In the silent night or in the morning light
Such a miracle

Azaleas drinking pale moonbeams
Gardenias floating through day dreams
No matter where you go
Wherever it may grow
A flower is a lovesome thing

INTERPRETATION

In his piano intro on his solo recording, Billy Strayhorn sets the tone with a mesmerizing pattern in the A section.

And on his recording with strings, he harmonizes the opening theme in triads in the right hand and adds fast fills using the C♭ Lydian dominant scale.

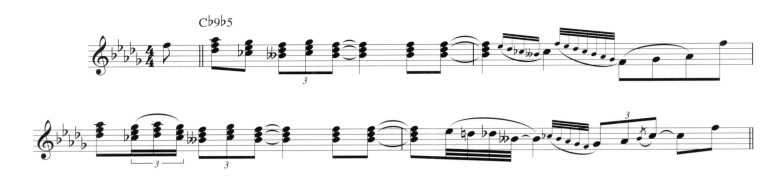

To illustrate the difficulty of identifying a definitive version of even the basic melody, this same recording includes Billy Strayhorn, during the bridge, playing a different note than most other versions, including another of his own.

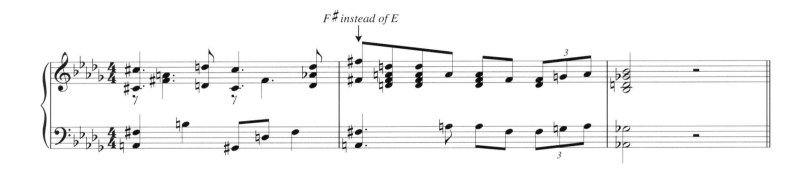

A version by Joe Henderson—on his tribute album *Lush Life*—casts the song as a duet with trumpet. During the A sections, Henderson's sax fills in the spaces between the opening theme statements, played by Wynton Marsalis, and then outlines the harmonic changes underneath the melody in measures 5–8.

A FLOWER IS A LOVESOME THING

By Billy Strayhorn

LUSH LIFE

Billy Strayhorn began writing "Lush Life" when he was a teenager, and completed the song in 1936.

FORM

This, one of his best-known and most cherished songs, is also one of his most unusual, complex, and astonishingly individual creations. "Lush Life" has an AB form, a verse-and-refrain lament typical of cabaret and theatre songs of the era. Rodgers and Hart's "He Was Too Good to Me" (1930) and Cole Porter's "Down in the Depths" (1936) are similar examples. The A and B sections of "Lush Life" are contrasting in tone: they tell of the before and after, and the subject is romance. The verse, a freely moving patter, introduces the song and establishes the setting: the cosmopolitan lifestyle among the "in" crowd, the *bon vivants*. The refrain is slower—sad and rueful, it represents the disillusionment of romance.

The music is structured following the phrasing of the lyrics, not the other way around. This results in unusual phrase lengths and an asymmetrical, episodic structure that still creates a satisfying balance.

The A section has two 14-measure sections, which taken together consist of four phrases: a1, a2, b1, and b2 with measure groupings of seven, seven, four, and ten, respectively, for a total of 28 measures.

The B section is divided into four phrases, with more traditional, even phrasing: a1, a2, b, and a3, each having four measures, for a total of 16 measures (8+8), plus an eight-measure coda (4+4), for a grand total of 24 measures.

The key formal element, musically speaking, is variation. A melodic motif is introduced, and the repetition of the motif leads to a new one through intervallic variation. The variation expands the intervals and rhythms as the motif spirals into longer phrases, eventually creating the form on a larger scale.

The song is seldom if ever played in a single tempo all the way through because of its episodic nature, with pauses, starts and stops, and points of emphasis. So, unlike most jazz standards, the song is seldom played with multiple solo choruses, but can include an instrumental solo by repeating the B section, with an instrumental solo for a portion of the section and the vocal entering for the coda.

LYRICS

"Lush Life" romanticizes a world of sophistication, money, jazz, and cocktail bars. With references to Paris and a sprinkling of French, the lyrics are an idealization of the penthouse lifestyle. At the same time, they manage to paint a portrait of loneliness and loss, rejection, and unfulfilled promise. This duality gives the song its two-part form.

Billy Strayhorn must have nurtured this idealized world in his imagination, as it was far from the gritty reality of Homewood in the 1920s, the poor, working-class area of Pittsburgh where he grew up. There is a similar theme in another of his most beautiful compositions, "Something to Live For," in a sense a companion piece to "Lush Life." The songs are remarkable for having been written by someone so young and with little if any direct experience of the world being described. Yet the same conundrum applies to the music: how could he have written such sophisticated songs at such a young age? Somehow he was able to take the songs he heard on the radio and what he learned from the sheet music and classical scores he had studied and create songs well beyond his experience.

The opening lyrics spotlight Strayhorn's inventive wordplay. His bold fusions like "twelve o'clocktails" and "troughful" show an eagerness and wit. The A section tumbles forward with inner rhymes in tight structures.

I used to visit all the very gay places,
Those come-what-may places,
Where one relaxes on the axis of the wheel of life
To get the feel of life
From jazz and cocktails.

The unusual elements working in this phrase are the added syllables and addition of the inner rhyme "relaxes-axis" in the third line, which otherwise matches the first line. The fifth line, standing on its own, throws off the couplet pattern and sets up the unpredictable structure of the song.

The second half of the song features abundant, playful alliteration: "life-lonely," "seemed-sure," "be-bore," "smile-spite," "burning-brain," "stifling-strive," "live-lush-life," and "rot-rest." And again, inner rhymes are tucked into the phrases: "Paris" and "care is," "forget you" and "while yet you."

The musical language in "Lush Life" matches the breezy high life as well as the loneliness described in the lyric. But how does the song manage to escape self-pity? The musical setting avoids cliché through constant invention, using chromatic variation as a means to explore the moods and feelings of pain and longing in a deep, personal way. And the lyrical choices are unique, with the phrase groupings idiosyncratic enough to sound improvised and free from formula. Like all good art, this has the paradoxical effect of being universal—we are able to join in the journey taken, touching on some of the deeper places we've all visited (disillusion, sorrow, and even anger), but refusing to wallow in these places. We can find some comfort, even humor, in imagining a place where we will not be alone in our loneliness.

MELODY

The melodic ideas closely follow the lyric's phrases, varying the motifs by expanding the intervals and letting the chromatic alterations lead to unexpected places.

Though firmly in the key of D♭ major, the melody explores three chromatic alterations of the major scale: the flat versions of the 3rd, 6th, and 7th degrees. Closely resembling parts of a blues scale, the altered notes lend a jazzy, bluesy feel to the melody.

These three altered notes will be used in remarkably creative ways throughout the melody, infusing it with a characteristic flavor, generating melodic motifs, and providing a means of venturing outside the home key.

The first two melodic phrases are nearly identical, climbing the altered scale and featuring note repetitions and a bluesy riff at the end.

The next phrase modulates to F minor, the minor iii, and flips the idea of the opening phrases by using a melodic minor scale, with a *raised* 6th scale degree.

The B section uses new material, but it is tied to the A section through the same three altered scale tones. Here, a motif is developed that works with a four-note cell, a pair of ascending and descending major 2nd intervals.

The motif is expanded chromatically, and the phrase comes to rest, temporarily, on the B♮. This is the enharmonic equivalent of the ♭7th, and as it returns to the opening motif via the ♭6th the melody returns using the same notes in the original cell.

On the next phrase, the melody takes a different path, expanding the line further to the ♭6th, A, to pivot and then drop down to C, setting up a parallel to the previous phrase, but up a half step.

The variations continue, with the motif now transposed to the V, again with the bluesy ♭7th, which takes the original four-note cell to A♭. The repetition of the phrase transposes the same motif to D, the ♭II of our home key. All of the permutations of the cell are marked.

The altered versions of the 3rd, 6th, and 7th degrees not only vary the melodic material within the context of the home key, but also lead to other keys and point the way to remote modulations.

Billy Strayhorn's melodic approach would grow more concise as time went on, but the signature characteristic of his harmonic approach stayed the same: parallel harmony. He loved to take complex 7th and 9th chords and set them in parallel motion, moving in half or whole steps, moving diatonically or chromatically.

Like the altered scale degrees used in the melody, the chromatic harmonies function as substitutes for diatonic harmonies, especially the tritone substitute, or as a mechanism for remote-key modulation. In "Lush Life" the harmony follows the melodic contours up the scale, pivoting on common tones to remote-key harmonies. Then we find the first example of the tritone substitution: substituting the ♭II for the V7 chord. This allows for more parallel movement in the harmony, which is avoided in the traditional V–I progression.

In the next phrase, as the harmony remains on F minor, the inner voice movement highlights the chromatic alterations of the 6th and 7th scale degrees that characterize the melody. And in a progression leading out of the A section, there is a continuation of the tritone substitution: ♭VII leading to VI7 (V7 of ii). The ii then leads to the V7 of the home key by way of the ♭VI, the tritone substitute for the ii. Notice how the chord roots create a line true to the altered scale of the melody: they, too, emphasize the ♭3rd, 6th, and 7th degrees.

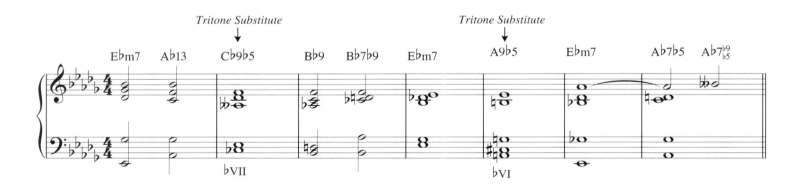

As the mood changes, the tempo slows, the B section begins, and we see an inversion of the chromatic pattern of the A-section harmony—now, I to ♭II.

The back-and-forth of this progression perfectly expresses the lyric: It's the sigh of disappointment, the stuck, back-where-I-started feeling, harmonized. Following the melody, half step variations lead to E major, as the harmonic pattern is extended chromatically to the V7, or B7. From there, it moves down in parallel harmony and chromatically back to D♭. Then, there's a move to F major, by way of a variation on the previous phrase, and another quick series of chromatically descending chords leads to the V7 of V.

And from V, a wonderful variation on the tritone substitution leads to ♭II (D), as the points of modulation outline the tritone substitution: V (A♭) of ♭II (D) to I (D♭.)

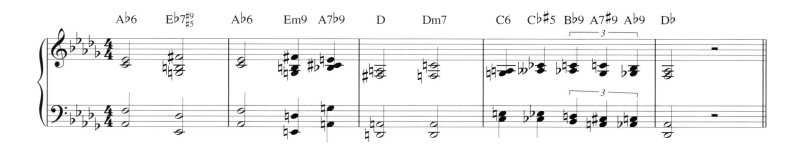

Leading into the coda, the reprise of the opening phrase of the B section leads to a climax on VI7, down from I. Even though this progression is quite common, it sounds so unusual here because the entire song has emphasized the parallel progressions of I–VII and I–♭II, and this is now harmonically fresh territory. Fittingly, this point is the climax of the B section.

The coda ends on what will become Billy Strayhorn's most unique and identifiable signatures: a chromatic melody, harmonized with rich 7th and 9th chords. The special feature here is the contrary motion of the melody and harmony. Before, they moved parallel, but here the chord voicings slowly descend as the melody ascends, with harmonic changes for every note of the melody.

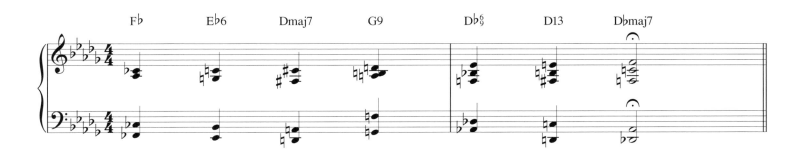

The rhythmic style of the song is "ad lib."—freely phrased, out of tempo and with stops, starts, and pauses for effect. The B section is sometimes done in-tempo, but inevitably the tempo slows, becoming freely expressive for the ending.

The rhythmic motion of the song is driven by the lyric. This style is often referred to as "colla voce," or "with the voice." This is an indication for the instrument(s) accompanying a singer to follow the rhythmic motion of that singer. This rhythm might move faster or slower at times, with elongations and other liberties taken in the interpretation of the printed rhythm, in order to communicate the meaning of the lyric.

In the A section, the eighth notes spin out restlessly into longer phrases, exploring and expanding the rhythmic patterns as they follow the natural rhythm of the syllables. The rhythms support the rhyme structure of the lyric, so "gay places" matches "may places," and "wheel of life" matches "feel of life."

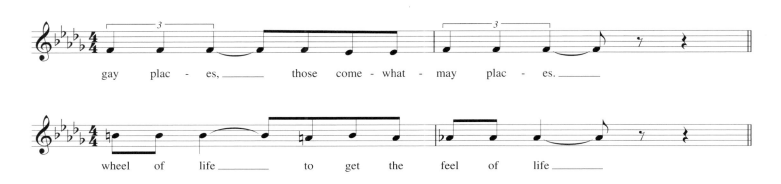

The most obvious change in the overall flow of the rhythm comes at the end of the A section, when slowing the tempo gives added weight to the final phrase, "again I was wrong."

As the B section begins, a steady rhythmic pulse is established. The opening measures are divided into two rhythmic groupings: four eighth notes and a quarter note triplet. The one-measure pattern, again following the rhythmic placement of the lyric, is a dotted quarter note followed by an eighth note, and then to the quarter note triplets. The triplets, combined with a slower, more deliberate tempo, broaden the rhythmic feel so the rhyming of the lyrics is drawn out, in contrast to the A section.

This "lengthening," created by subdividing beats 3 and 4 into the three-note triplet, underlines and exaggerates the lyrics and achieves the contrast necessary in distinguishing the chatty, breezy A section and the deeply felt, resigned quality of the B section.

This pattern continues until the coda, where the steady beat and triplet rhythm give way to a return of the freer, eighth note motion. Here, a more volatile style helps accent the disillusion. Billy Strayhorn's recording demonstrates the way the piano accompaniment can add rhythm to accent the vocal interpretation.

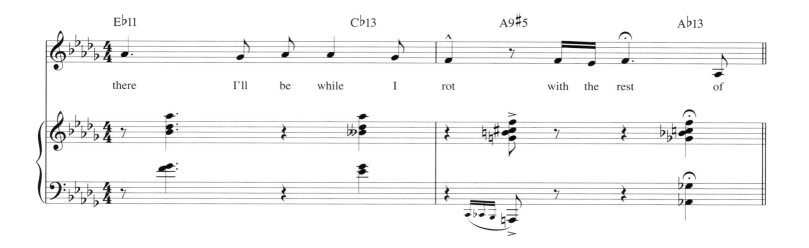

INTERPRETATION

One of the notable exceptions to the accepted wisdom of singing the melody as written is in taking the last note of the A section an octave down, as Ella Fitzgerald and Johnny Hartman do.

Joe Pass, in his lovely accompaniment to his duet with Ella Fitzgerald, plays some beautiful chord substitutions for the last two measures (performed in the key of A major).

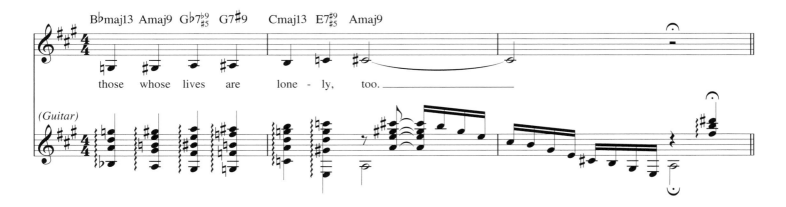

Sarah Vaughan does a nice variation to the ending using expanding intervals, sketching out the harmonies and elongating the vowels. Queen Latifah also does this on her more recent recording.

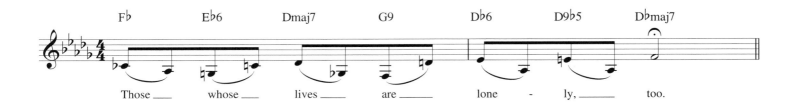

In his recording with Johnny Hartmann, John Coltrane's tenor sax solo starts with an eight-measure vamp (in double time) over the I–♭II7 chords, continuing on through the B section to the coda, where the vocal comes in again and the original tempo resumes.

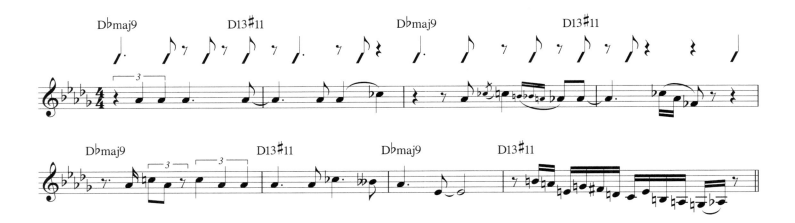

Roland Hanna's solo piano joins Strayhorn and Debussy in a "Claire de Lune"–style setting.

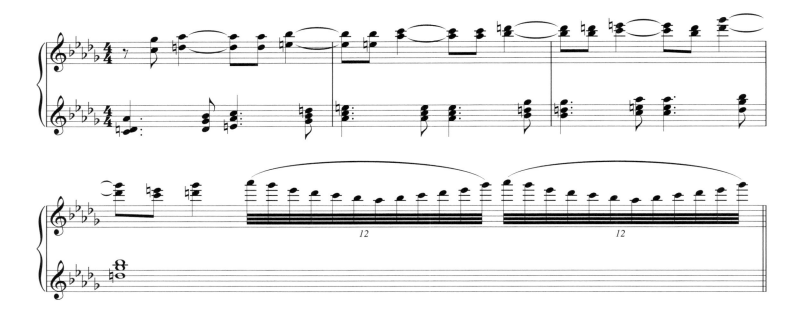

LUSH LIFE

By Billy Strayhorn

girls I knew had sad and sul - len gray fac - es, ____ with dis - tin - gué trac - es ____ that used to be there, you could see where they'd been washed a - way ____ by too man - y through-the - day twelve o' - clock tails. Then you came a - long with your si - ren song to tempt me to mad - ness, ____

I thought for a while that your poig - nant smile was

tinged with the sad - ness of a great love for me. _____

Ah, yes, I was wrong, a - gain I was

wrong! _____ Life is lone - ly a -

gain, and on - ly last year ev - 'ry - thing seemed so

sure. Now life is aw - ful a - gain, a trough - ful of

hearts could on - ly be a bore. A week in Par - is will

ease the bite of it. All I care is to smile in spite of it.

More Great Piano/Vocal Books

FROM CHERRY LANE

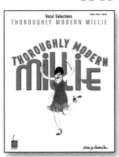

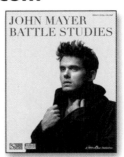

For a complete listing of Cherry Lane titles available,
including contents listings, please visit our web site at
www.cherrylane.com

See your local music dealer or contact:

7777 W. BLUEMOUND RD. P.O. BOX 13819 MILWAUKEE, WI 53213

Prices, contents and availability subject to change without notice.

0310